Biblical Training
Training for Gaining
Thomas Couch

The Spotted Feather

Dedication

I would like to dedicate this book to the readers. I would also like to dedicate it to my Precious Mother and all of my family. And with all due gratitude I would like to dedicate it to every person that is involved in the ministries worldwide. For their hard work, dedication, and love and kindness to all of those who sought the LORD, and found HIM as a result of the many great ministries out there.

May GOD bless you all beyond measure.

Sincerely in Christ,

Thomas Couch

REVIVE - ALL MINISTRIES

ISAIAH 57:15

Table of Contents

Introduction

This curriculum is designed for those who are seeking a deeper walk with GOD and a deeper look at Spiritual insight into everyday Biblical living.

The Course goes from learning how to rightly divide and rightly apply GOD'S WORD for everyday Biblical living to enjoying the Benefits, Rewards, and Blessings of everyday Biblical living.

The course includes:

1. Rightly dividing and applying GOD'S WORD;

2. Prayer in everyday Biblical living;

3. How to conduct our lives in everyday Biblical living;

4. Spiritual Warfare in everyday Biblical living.

5. Overcoming Situations and Circumstances daily;

6. Enjoying Benefits, Rewards, and Blessings daily;

7. Being Sure in everyday Biblical living;

8. Being Secure in everyday Biblical living;

9. Being Mature in everyday Biblical living.

The course is designed to prayerfully be fun and interesting for the participants as they grow in the Spiritual Insight into everyday Biblical living that has been provided throughout the 6-week study course, based on one session per week for six weeks.

Prayerfully the course will be a stepping stone into a deeper and richer relationship and walk with GOD for the church leaders and the participants.

In Christ's Service,

Evangelist/Author: Thomas Couch

All Scripture is from the New King James Version of the Bible.

Study Questions included.

Week 1

Rightly Dividing and Rightly Applying God's Word

TRAINING FOR GAINING

Have participants turn to all scripture.

Spiritual Insight into everyday Biblical Living

OPENING PRAYER

Open for discussion/input.

Action verses: Putting GOD'S Word into action in our lives for everyday Biblical living.

Be diligent to present yourself approved to GOD, a worker who does not need to be ashamed, rightly dividing the word of truth. (2nd TIMOTHY 2:15)

FOR GOD'S people it is one thing to "RIGHTLY DIVIDE" GOD'S word, but it is altogether another thing to "RIGHTLY APPLY" GOD'S word.

1. Because you have "Good Doctrine" and "Bad Doctrine." Some people will go as far as to say that "Bad Doctrine" is doctrines of demons. Whereas if we "RIGHTLY DIVIDE" GOD'S word for good and "RIGHTLY APPLY" it that way our light will shine. (PROVERBS 4:2, 1st TIMOTHY 4:1)

2. Train up a child in the way he should go, and when he is old, he will not depart from it.

Rightly dividing and rightly applying GOD'S Word for life.

Once we begin to rightly apply GOD'S word in our lives, we begin to see benefits and rewards.

Always be sure, secure, and mature when rightly applying GOD'S word.

1. The Apostle Paul asked for prayer to speak GOD'S word with mature boldness. (EPHESIANS 6:18-20)

2. Paul also said that when he was a child that he did childish things, but when he became a man, that he put away childish things. (1st CORINTHIANS 13:11)

Rightly divide.

Rightly apply for good.

Be sure.

Be secure.

Be mature.

Be diligent to present yourself approved to GOD, a worker who does not need to be ashamed, rightly dividing the word of truth. (2nd TIMOTHY 2:15)

CLOSING PRAYER

CLOSING DISCUSSION

Week # 1

Study Questions

1. How do you rightly divide GOD'S word?

2. How do you rightly apply GOD'S word?

3. Will you try to rightly divide GOD'S word in every situation you encounter?

4. Will you try to rightly apply GOD'S word in every situation you encounter?

5. Will you be sure when rightly dividing and applying GOD'S Word as you stand in faith?

6. Will you be secure when rightly dividing and applying GOD'S Word as you stand in faith?

7. Will you be mature when rightly dividing and applying GOD'S Word, knowing that GOD will do what HIS word says HE will do?

Week 2
Prayer

TRAINING FOR GAINING

Have participants turn to all scripture.

Spiritual Insight into everyday Biblical Living

OPENING PRAYER

Open for discussion/input.

Action verses: Putting GOD'S Word into action in our lives for everyday Biblical living.

And whatever you do in word or deed, do all in the name of the Lord Jesus, giving thanks to GOD the Father through HIM. Whatever we do in "WORD OR DEED" including prayer, we must do in the name of Jesus. (COLOSSIANS 3:17)

Prayer - Is indeed a part of everyday Biblical living.

Rightly dividing and rightly applying GOD'S Word in prayer.

Be diligent to present yourself approved to GOD, a worker who does not need to be ashamed, rightly dividing the word of truth. (2nd TIMOTHY 2:15)

Rightly dividing and rightly applying GOD'S WORD in prayer is the only way to get through to GOD.

The word of GOD TELLS US that we can ask "IN JESUS' NAME" and THE FATHER will give us what we ask for. (JOHN 14:14; 16:23-24; 15:7)

Actually, JOHN 15:7 says if HIS words abide in us, "in our prayers, then we can ask and it will be done for us."

Be sure, secure, and mature in knowing that GOD will answer your prayers when you have based your prayers on GOD'S promises from HIS word. AND YOU HAVE ASKED IN JESUS' NAME.

When the Apostle Paul asked for prayer to speak GOD'S Word boldly, (EPHESIANS 6:18-20) he was sure, secure, and mature, trusting that GOD would answer those prayers, and we can see from his other writings that GOD did because he spoke with such boldness that people didn't like him for it. And don't be surprised if the same things don't arise in your lives when you speak GOD'S Word with SURE, SECURE AND MATURE FAITH.

1. Do all in prayer IN THE NAME OF JESUS.

2. Rightly divide and rightly apply GOD'S WORD in prayer.

3. Be sure in prayer.

4. Be secure in prayer.

5. Be mature in prayer.

And whatever you do in WORD OR DEED, do all in the name of the Lord Jesus, giving thanks to GOD the Father through HIM. (COLOSSIANS 3:17)

CLOSING PRAYER

DISCUSSION

Week # 2

Study Questions

1. Do you think that praying is part of everyday Biblical living?

2. Do you feel like you rightly divide GOD'S Word for your prayers?

3. Do you feel like you rightly apply GOD'S Word in your prayers?

4. Do you feel like if you rightly divide and apply GOD'S Word to your prayers, that GOD will answer them?

5. Are you sure in your prayers?

6. Are you secure without doubt while standing in faith for your prayers to be answered?

7. Are you mature in your prayers knowing that what you prayed is GOD'S Will?

Week 3
How We Conduct Our Lives

TRAINING FOR GAINING

Have participants turn to all scripture.

Spiritual Insight into everyday Biblical Living

OPENING PRAYER

Open for discussion/input.

Action verses: Putting GOD'S Word into action in our lives for everyday Biblical living.

These things I write to you, though I hope to come to you shortly; but if I am delayed, I write so that you may know how you ought to conduct yourself in the house of GOD, which is the Church of the living GOD, the pillar and ground of the truth. (1st TIMOTHY 3:14-15)

FOR GOD'S PEOPLE: We must conduct our lives in a Godly manner in the house of GOD. That means that we must be able to rightly divide and rightly apply GOD'S WORD to our everyday lives. (2nd TIMOTHY 2:15)

We must be able to walk in love. (EPHESIANS 5:2) Because love never fails. (1st CORINTHIANS 13:8 a.)

We should also walk in newness of life. (ROMANS 6:4)

We should also walk by faith and not by sight. (2nd CORINTHIANS 5:7)

We also should not walk in the counsel of the ungodly, that means that we shouldn't be led by ungodly people in the way that we conduct our lives, but we should be led by GOD'S WORD and THE HOLY SPIRIT. (PSALMS 1:1-3)

We must always be sure, secure, and mature in our conduct and the way that we conduct our lives, not just in the house of GOD, but everywhere that we go.

1. We must maintain Godly conduct.

2. We must be able to rightly divide and rightly apply GOD'S Word in love in our conduct.

3. We must be sure in our conduct.

4. We must be secure in our conduct.

5. We must be mature in our conduct.

These things I write to you, though I hope to come to you shortly; but if I am delayed, I write so that you may know how you ought to conduct yourself in the house of GOD, which is the Church of the living GOD, the pillar and ground of the truth. (1st TIMOTHY 3:14-15)

CLOSING PRAYER

CLOSING DISCUSSION

Week # 3

Study Questions

1. Do you believe that the word of GOD teaches how we should conduct our lives in the house of GOD?

2. Do you believe that we should conduct our lives in the same manner outside the house of GOD?

3. Do you think it would have an effect on our testimony if we lived differently outside the Church than we do while in Church?

4. It should be enjoyable to walk in love. Is it enjoyable for you?

5. Which shows most in your life, the old you or your newness of life?

6. Do you enjoy walking by faith and not by sight?

7. Do you believe it is important to maintain a Godly conduct all of the time?

Week 4
Spiritual Warfare

TRAINING FOR GAINING

Have participants turn to all scripture.

Spiritual Insight into everyday Biblical Living

OPENING PRAYER

Open for discussion/input.

Action verses: Putting GOD'S Word into action in our lives for everyday Biblical living.

Finally, my brethren, be strong in the Lord and in the power of his might. (EPHESIANS 6:10)

FOR GOD'S PEOPLE Spiritual warfare is without a doubt a part of everyday Biblical living. Here GOD'S people are urged to be strong in the Lord and the power of HIS might during times of Spiritual warfare and not trust in our own strength. (EPHESIANS 6:10-17; EPHESIANS 6:17)

Knowing how to rightly divide and rightly apply GOD'S WORD during times of Spiritual warfare is very important for GOD'S people. (2nd TIMOTHY 2:15; EPHESIANS 6:17)

GOD'S people must be able to stand against evil and always remember that the battle is not flesh and blood; in other words, the battle is not against people, but against Spiritual forces.

Thus, GOD'S people must remain strong in the Lord and the power of HIS might and love the people involved but not the Spirits that we battle against. (EPHESIANS 6:10; 1st CORINTHIANS 16:13-14)

GOD'S people must always be sure, secure, and mature during times of Spiritual warfare. (EPHESIANS 6:10-17; EPHESIANS 6:18-20)

1. We must be strong in the Lord in Spiritual warfare.

2. We must be able to rightly divide and rightly apply GOD'S WORD during Spiritual warfare.

3. We must be sure in Spiritual warfare.

4. We must be secure in Spiritual warfare.

5. We must be mature in Spiritual warfare.

Finally, my brethren, be strong in the Lord and in the power of HIS might.

CLOSING PRAYER

CLOSING DISCUSSION

Week # 4

Study Questions

1. Do you believe it is important to be strong in the Lord and the Power of HIS might?

2. Do you believe that the Power of the Lord is strong enough to help you win any battle?

3. How do you view Spiritual warfare?

4. Do you believe that you sometimes encounter situations where Spiritual warfare is necessary?

5. Do you believe that you need to know how to rightly divide and rightly apply GOD'S WORD in Spiritual warfare?

6. Do you have trouble loving others when they do things you disagree with?

7. Do you believe it is important to love the person and rebuke the Spirit behind the scene when people do you wrong?

Week 5
Overcoming Obstacles

TRAINING FOR GAINING

Have participants turn to all scripture.

Spiritual Insight into everyday Biblical Living

OPENING PRAYER

Open for discussion/input.

Action verses: Putting GOD'S Word into action in our lives for everyday Biblical living.

And take the helmet of Salvation, and the sword of the Spirit, which is the word of God. (EPHESIANS 6:17)

Using the sword of the Spirit, GOD'S WORD and being strong in the Lord and HIS might and speaking to our "giants," situations and circumstances are indeed a part of everyday Biblical living, because GOD'S people continuously have situations and circumstances arise in our everyday lives. (EPHESIANS 6:10; EPHESIANS 6:17)

When we have to use the sword of the Spirit, GOD'S WORD, to speak to our situations and circumstances we "HAVE" to be able to rightly divide and rightly apply the word of GOD to have victory over these situations and circumstances. (2nd TIMOTHY 2:15; EPHESIANS 6:17)

Let's say that our situation or circumstance is <u>sickness</u>.

We must always speak the solution from GOD'S WORD.

If it is sickness, we need to speak verses like these so that healing will come.

(EXODUS 23:25; PSALMS 103:1-3; JEREMIAH 30:17)

Let's say that our situation or circumstance is <u>financial need, supply or any other kind of need</u>.

We must always speak the solution from GOD'S WORD.

If it is financial need, we should speak verses like these:

(DEUTERONOMY 28:1-14; PSALMS 1:1-3; PSALMS 112:1-3; JOHN 10:10 b)

If it is any other need, we should speak verses like these:

(MATTHEW 6:8; PHILIPPIANS 4:19)

Let's say that our situation or circumstance involves <u>relationship issues</u>.

We must always speak the solution from GOD'S WORD.

If it involves relationships, we must speak verses like these:

(JOHN 15:12; EPHESIANS 4:2-3; COLOSSIANS 3:13; GALATIANS 6:2)

We must always be sure, secure, and mature when speaking to our situations and circumstances so that we can win the victory over them.

1. We must have the sword of the Spirit when speaking to our situations and circumstances.

2. We must be able to rightly divide and rightly apply the sword of the Spirit when speaking to our situations and circumstances.

3. We must be sure when speaking to our situations and circumstances.

4. We must be secure when speaking to our situations and circumstances.

5. We must be mature when speaking to our situations and circumstances.

And take the helmet of Salvation, and the sword of the Spirit, which is the Word of GOD. (EPHESIANS 6:17)

CLOSING PRAYER

CLOSING DISCUSSION

Week # 5

Study Questions

1. Do you believe that GOD'S Word has power?

2. Do you speak GOD'S Word into your life, and situations that you encounter?

3. Do you believe that there is a solution in GOD'S Word for any kind of situation that you may encounter in your life?

4. Do you believe that GOD will move in your situations if you pray and speak HIS word in those situations?

5. Do you believe that GOD'S Word has the power you need to live in victory? (HEBREWS 4:12)

6. Do you believe that it is important to study and know GOD'S Word before we encounter situations where it is needed?

7. Do you want to study GOD'S Word more now that you know how important it is for you to know it?

Week 6
Benefits, Rewards and Blessings

TRAINING FOR GAINING

Have participants turn to all scripture.

Spiritual Insight into everyday Biblical Living

OPENING PRAYER

Open for discussion/input.

Action verses: Putting GOD'S Word into action in our lives for everyday Biblical living.

Blessed be the God and Father of our Lord Jesus Christ, who has blessed us with every spiritual blessing in the heavenly places in Christ. (EPHESIANS 1:3)

Once we begin to rightly divide and rightly apply GOD'S WORD to our lives we begin to receive Benefits, Rewards, and Blessings in our lives in every area of our lives in every day Biblical living. (PSALMS 103:1-5; HEBREWS 11:6; EPHESIANS 1:3)

PSALMS 103:1-5 Specifically says "Bless the Lord, O my soul; And all that is within me bless His holy name; Bless the Lord, O my soul, and forget not all His Benefits; Who forgives all your iniquities, who heals all your diseases, who redeems your life from destruction, who crowns you with loving-kindness and tender mercies, who satisfies your mouth with good things, so that your youth is renewed like the eagle's. (PSALMS 103:1-5)

The WORD OF GOD also says "Now he who plants and he who waters are one, and each one will receive his own reward according to his own labor." (1st CORINTHIANS 3:8) The WORD OF GOD also says, "But without faith it is impossible to please Him, for he who comes to God must believe that He is, and that He is a rewarder of those who diligently seek Him. (HEBREWS 11:6)

GOD'S people can pretty much enjoy blessings in every area of our lives in everyday Biblical living. (EPHESIANS 1:3; PSALMS 1:1-3; PSALMS 112:1-3; DEUTERONOMY 28:1-14; JOHN 10:10 b.)

The WORD OF GOD actually says, But as it is written; "Eye has not seen, nor ear heard, The things which God has prepared for those who love Him. (1st CORINTHIANS 2:9)

Thus, we can be sure, secure, and mature in everyday Biblical living "KNOWING" that we have received benefits, rewards and blessings in pretty much every area of our lives. (EPHESIANS 1:3)

1. Enjoy spiritual blessings in every area in everyday Biblical living.

2. Enjoy rewards and benefits in every area in everyday Biblical living.

3. Be sure in your joyful everyday Biblical living.

4. Be secure in your joyful everyday Biblical living.

5. Be mature in your joyful everyday Biblical living.

Blessed be the God and Father of our LORD JESUS CHRIST, who has blessed us with every spiritual blessing in the heavenly places in Christ. (EPHESIANS 1:3)

CLOSING PRAYER

CLOSING DISCUSSION

Week # 6

Study Questions

1. Do you believe that you will receive benefits if you rightly divide and rightly apply GOD'S Word to your life?

2. Do you believe that there are rewards for rightly dividing and rightly applying GOD'S Word to your life?

3. Do you believe that you will be blessed if you rightly divide and rightly apply GOD'S Word to your life?

4. Do you have fun and enjoy living for the LORD?

5. Does it make you want to study GOD'S Word more to know that it will benefit you and others?

6. Are you willing to tell others of the goodness of GOD so they can be blessed like you are?

7. How has this 6-week Bible study course impacted your life?

Power Prayer

For Salvation and to be baptized in the Holy Spirit.

Father GOD, I come to you as humbly as I know how. Lord, your word says in 1st JOHN 1:9, "If we confess our sins, he is faithful and just to forgive us our sins, and to cleanse us from all unrighteousness." So, I confess to you that I have sinned in many ways. I now repent and turn away from my sins and I ask you to forgive me and cleanse me from all of my unrighteousness, in the name of Jesus.

Father, your word also says in ROMANS 10:9-10, "That if thou shalt confess with thy mouth the Lord Jesus, and shalt believe in thine heart that God raised him from the dead, thou shalt be saved. For with the heart man believeth into righteousness; and with the mouth confession is made unto salvation."

So I confess with my mouth that I believe Jesus died on the Cross so I can be saved and I believe with all my heart that GOD raised HIM from the dead and I ask you to come into my life and save me. I now accept Jesus as my Lord and Savior and I believe with all my heart that your word is true and that I am saved by grace!

Father, your word also says in the book of LUKE 11:13, "If ye then being evil, know how to give good gifts unto your children: how much more shall your heavenly Father give the Holy Spirit to them that ask him?"

So Father, I ask you to give me the gift of the Holy Spirit. I ask you to fill me till my cup runs over and allow me to successfully function in the gifts of the Spirit that are mentioned in your word. So that I become an effective witness for Jesus and a blessing to others for the rest of my life. In Jesus' name I pray, Amen!

If you prayed this prayer, you can believe without a doubt that you are saved. The Bible says, "you shall be saved." That is a promise and it is also a promise that GOD will fill you with the Holy Spirit if you ask HIM.

So now you need to join a good Church and sincerely turn away from your old sinful life and walk in and enjoy the new Spirit filled life that GOD has given you. The old you should start fading into the past and the new you will start shining brightly as you seek to serve GOD in all that you do.

About the Author

Thomas Couch has a GED, and some college credits (no degree) with MERCER, and BREWTON PARKER Universities. He was an Honor Roll Student while he attended College.

The name of his ministry is "REVIVE-ALL" Ministries. This Ministry is an outreach of "Souls Harbor Word of Faith Church" in Canton, Georgia where he was ordained and licensed to minister as a Preacher of The Gospel. He has a Certificate for "Caring for People God's Way" with Light University, that is approved by the American Association of Christian Counselors Board.

He is currently a member of "Colorful Crow Writers Community" and he is engaged in a writing ministry.

GOD gave Thomas this material to write in efforts to minister to GOD'S People, to reach the lost, and to abundantly bless all who will enjoy its contents. He says it is proof that with GOD you can do all things through Christ who strengthens you. (PHILIPPIANS 4:13)

He prays it will be a blessing to everyone it reaches.

www.ingramcontent.com/pod-product-compliance
Lightning Source LLC
Chambersburg PA
CBHW061329120626
46546CB00007B/2731